FAITH
VS FEAR

FAITH
VS FEAR

HOPE FOR TODAY

*Biography included
in The Marquis
Who's Who in America*

DR. JOAN A. POLIDORE

ReadersMagnet, LLC

TABLE OF CONTENTS

PREFACE

The Bible's definitions of fear include entries such as: "Be not wise in your own eyes; fear the Lord and depart from evil. The fear of the Lord is the beginning of wisdom, and the knowledge of the holy one is understanding" (Pro. 9:10). "The fear of the Lord is the instruction of wisdom and before honor is humility" (Pro.15:33). "There is no fear in love but perfect love cast out fear because fear has punishment first" (John 4:1).

Fear is the basic instinct of every living thing. An animal without fear will probably become some predator's dinner. Fear is a natural response whenever physical safety and even psychological well-being of a being are threatened. Rational fears are learned and vital for our survival.

The difference between anxiety and fear is that anxiety lacks an object or adequate cause. People are anxious because they are uncertain about a specific outcome or don't know what is going to happen in the future. It is imperative to distinguish between temporary anxiety and an anxious trait that continues on and on.

There are various types of fears:
A fear of crowds, claustrophobia;
Fear of heights, acrophobia;
Fear of spiders, arachnophobia.
These can lead to a panic attack in certain persons. There are also:
Fear of God, reverential fear, to obey and honor God;
Fear of man, that possessed by man pleasers;
Fear of death;
Fear of failure.

CHAPTER 1:
FAITH VERSUS FEAR

WHAT IS FAITH?

FAITH: Belief in or confident attitude towards God, involving commitment to His will for one's life – that's true! FAITH is confidence in God or Christ, not in oneself.

FAITH is part of the Christian life from beginning to end. As the instrument by which the gift of salvation is received (Eph.2:8-9), faith is thus distinct from the basis of salvation, which is grace.

FAITH comes by hearing, and hearing by the word of God (Rom.10:17). "Let the Word of Christ dwell in your heart richly" (Col.3:16). "If you abide in me and my words abide in you, you shall ask what you will, and it shall be done unto you" (John 15:7). WHEN FEAR COMES, THE SHIELD OF FAITH WILL DRIVE IT AWAY.

God's good book indicates, "Above all, [take] the shield of faith, wherewith you shall be able to quench all the fiery darts of the wicked" (Eph. 6:16).

"Faith can cause us to be of good cheer in the midst of the storm. God is right there with us" (Isa.41:10).

We are advised, "Fear thou not; for I am with thee, be not dismayed; for I am thy God: I will strengthen thee; yea, I will help thee; yea, I will uphold thee with the right hand of my righteousness. God bids us cast all our cares upon Him for He cares for us. You shall ask what you will, and it shall be done unto you" (John 15:7).

Whether we have great faith or little faith, they both glorify God; "For without faith it is impossible to please God, for he that comes to God must believe and that He is a rewarder of them that diligently seek Him" (Hebrews 11:6). The woman with the little faith went out and gave her testimony. The community came and accepted Jesus as their Messiah (John 4:28). The woman with the great faith went to start a church in Tyre and Sidon (Matt.15:21). She exercise her faith and did what her faith allowed. Likewise the woman with the great faith she did what her Faith allowed her to do. She built a church. Teaching us that, we should not envy anyone fore what they have but use what we have for the glory of God.

A perfect example of faith is "When the disciples saw that the fig tree had withered away, which Jesus had commanded for no fruit to grow on after that day, they marveled, saying, 'How soon is the fig tree withered away!' Jesus said to them, 'Verily I say unto you, if you have faith, and doubt not, you shall not only do this which is done to the fig tree, but also if you shall say unto this mountain, Be thou removed, and be thou cast into the sea; it shall be done'" (Matt.21:21). You see faith like a grain of mustard seed can remove mountains. Jesus said this to give credence to the old adage, "Faith can move mountains," hence, "What things so-ever you desire, when you pray, believe that you receive them, and you shall have them" (Mark 11:22-24).

We ought to believe in God. "If we believe not, yet He abideth faithful: He cannot deny Himself" (2 Timothy 2:12). He will grant us the desires of our hearts. "For He opens His hands and satisfies the desire of every living soul" (Psalms 145:16). During Peter's challenge on the sea to attempt to meet Jesus, he made two cries; one was for victory, for he was really walking on water. The second cry was for despair because he took his eyes off Jesus and was sinking. However, the omniscient God heard both cries and satisfied them each! The God of all comfort comforted the heart in despair. The triumphant God encouraged him that he could do all things through Christ, who strengthened him (Phil.4:13). There are the same among "fear not" as there are of "be of good cheer" in the Bible; that is because the Devil, the accuser of the brethren, uses fear to get us to doubt the word of God.

With faith comes hope. Jacabed had enough hope and confidence in her God that she defiled the king's command and saved her son instead of allowing fear to dictate the destiny of the "Leader and Deliver" God had given her to protect for that short period of time with adversities.

In life, we are faced with adversities such as death in the family, divorce, loss of jobs, loss of houses, etc.; yet we can be confident that the Lord, our God in the midst of us, is mighty. "Many are the afflictions of the righteous, but the Lord delivereth us out of them all (Psalm 34:19)." "Though plagues, pestilence, and famine may strike we have a blessed hope." (Romans 5:1-5) "Therefore being justified by faith, we have peace with God through our Lord Jesus Christ.....And hope maketh not ashamed; because the love of God is shed abroad in our hearts by the Holy Ghost which is given to us".

There is no disappointment in "hope" but a glorious assurance that to be absent from the body is to be present with God. Greater yet, Jesus is coming back to take us to live with Him forever - no more pains, no more sorrow. And God shall wipe away all tears from their eyes, and there shall be no more death: for the former things are passed away (Rev.21:4).

During the Apostle Paul's voyage to Rome, in that great storm, he encouraged the sailors to hold on to the broken pieces, for there was "hope." Paul gave us much confidence in "hope" because of the hope that Jesus is soon to return for His bride, the Church. None of these things shall separate us from the love of God (Rom.8:35).

God has a purpose in permitting wicked men to rule. He has set a time in which He will judge the wicked deeds of ungodly men, for he has divine control in the affairs of men on earth. God said to Pharaoh, "I will show my power in you, that my name may be declared in all the earth." "Having disarmed principalities and powers, He made a public spectacle of them, triumphing over them in it" (Col.2:15). In virtue of the triumphant victory, we can say thanks be to God, who gives us the victory through our Lord Jesus Christ. Jesus' resurrection is the guarantee of our blessed hope. "Christ in us [is] the hope of glory" (Col.1:27).

FAITH TRIUMPH OVER FEAR

"Jesus is the resurrection and the life, he who believes in Me, though he may die, shall live" (John 11:25). And by believing in Him, we have life and life more abundantly. We have victory over death, sorrow, and pain. In spite of the plight of life, we are more than conquerors through Christ, who loves us and gave His life a ransom for us.

FAITH VERSUS FEAR: FAITH CONQUERS FEAR.

No one is exempted from fear. As a Christian, I was afraid to drive to my church because there was a hill to climb. But one summer, I had to teach Vacation Bible School, so I prayed, and I asked God to deliver me from that spirit of fear because I wanted to teach Vacation Bible School, since it is my passion My Faith in God allowed me to believe that through prayer, I would be delivered from my fear. One Sunday, I told my husband to sit in the car with me while I drove down THIS hill. When I got to the bottom of the hill, I was surprised that I had miraculously overcame my fear that had intimidated me for years (1John 2:14-15). I had the confidence that God had answered my prayers and given me victory over fear. I was overwhelmed that I could now drive up and down that hill whenever I wanted.

Fear is an emotion that causes us to focus on the situation rather than redirecting our attitude towards God, who has given us the spirit of adoption whereby we cry, "Abba Father." Once Peter was sure it was Jesus in the boat, he walked towards Him. But when he doubted, he began to sink. Trust will cause us to triumph over our trials. Faith will cause us to persevere in spite of our challenges.

Jesus already knew that Peter would sink as long as he focused on his ability, "I am the vine; you are the branches. He who abides in Me, and I in Him, bears much fruit, for without me, you can do nothing" (John 15:5). Jesus encouraged Peter to exercise his faith by telling him to come. God knows our ability; He just wants us to be obedient and trust Him. When He called Jeremiah, he said "Oh, I am a child, I cannot speak." This was God's answer to him: "Before you were born, I sanctified you; I ordained you a prophet to the nations. Before I formed you in the womb I knew you" (Jer. 1:5). Jeremiah was speaking to the only true and wise God.

Our failure in life is our focus: "VISION DOMINATES LIFE" (Pro. 11:30, 27:23). Elisha prayed and said, "Lord, I pray thee, open his eyes that he may see." And the Lord opened the eyes of the young man, and he saw, and behold: the mountain was full of horses and chariots of fire all around Elisha (2 Kings 6:17). If we keep our eyes on the storm, then we will sink, but victory is ours by trusting the master of the storm, (Matt. 14:31). When Peter cried, God heard him. God is right there with us. With the widow whose only son died, "And when the Lord saw her, he had compassion on her and said unto her weep not" (Luke 7:13).

WHAT IS FEAR?

According to the Bible, fear has torment. "There is no fear in love, but perfect love casteth out fear; because fear has torment. He that feareth is not made perfect in love" (1 John 4:18). For we have not received the spirit of bondage again to fear, but the spirit of adoption, whereby we cry "Abba Father." The disciples on the Sea of Galilee encountered a severe storm, but when they saw Jesus walking on the sea, they were troubled, saying it was a spirit, and they cried out for fear. But straightaway, Jesus spoke unto them, saying, "Be of good cheer; it is I, be not afraid" (Matt.14;24-25).

When Abraham sent Hagar and her son away in the wilderness, God heard the voice of the boy, and He sent an angel to comfort them. The angel of God called to Hagar out of heaven and said to her, "What ails you, Hagar? Fear not, for God has heard the voice of the lad where he is. Arise and hold him with your hand, for I will make him a great nation" (Gen.21:16-18). It does not matter where we are; God sees and hears our cry. "For His eyes are upon the righteous, and His ears are open unto our cry" (Psalm.34:15).

When the disciples were on the sea, they were afraid because they did not yet come to the full understanding of who God is - master of the storm; everything He created serves a purpose to glorify Him, and therefore, we must obey Him (Rev.4:11). Thou art worthy, O Lord, to receive glory and honor and power, for thou hast created all things created, and for thy pleasure they are and were created. Jesus spoke to the fig tree, commanding it never to bear fruits anymore, releasing it from its baroness, from now on, henceforward, forever.

Jesus gave this authority to His disciples. "And I will give you the keys of the kingdom, and whatsoever you bind on earth shall be bound in heaven; and whatsoever you lose on earth shall be lost in heaven" (Matt.16:18). Elias prayed earnestly that it might not rain, and it rained not for three and a half years, so he prayed again, and the heaven gave rain, and the earth brought her fruits (James 5:17-18).

God has divine control in the affairs of men. There are many devices in the hearts of men, [notwithstanding] the counsel of the Lord that shall stand" (Pro.21:19). At the wedding at Cana, the host ran out of wine, and the mother of Jesus said to Him, "They have no wine" (John 2:3). Here, Jesus demonstrated His authority over creation because He is the Creator. "For by Him all things were created" (Col.1:16). Nature takes time to turn water into wine. Only God who created all things and established the laws of nature could instantly duplicate the process of nature by turning water into wine. It was a perfect vintage, created by the omnipotent God.

CHRIST'S AUTHORITY: He taught them as one having authority, not as the scribes (Matt.7:29). "And Jesus came and spoke unto them, saying, 'All power is given to me in heaven and earth'" (Matt. 28:18).

HIS IMMUTABILITY: "Of old hast thou laid the foundation of the heavens, which are the works of thy hands" (Ps.102:25). But the day of the Lord will come as a thief in the night, in the which the heavens shall pass away with a great noise, and the elements shall melt with fervent heat;, the earth also and the works therein shall be burnt up (2Pet.3:10). "For I am the Lord, I change not, therefore you sons of Jacob are not consumed" (Mal. 3:6).

"I am Alpha and Omega, the beginning and the ending, sayeth the Lord which is, and which was, and which is, to come the Almighty."

GOD ETERNAL: The Eternal God is our refuge, and underneath are the everlasting arms; and He shall thrust out the enemy from before thee and shall say, "Destroy them" (De.33:27). Jesus in His eternal glory has spoiled principalities and powers; he made a shew of them openly, triumphing over them in it, and is coming back in a like manner with power and glory (Col.2:15).

HUMANITY: Jesus was testing the obedience and confidence of the disciples in Him and whether they recognized Him. After a night fishing, and having caught no fish, Jesus said to them, "Cast the net on the right side of the boat, and you will find some" (John 21:6-7). So they cast their nets, and now they were not able to draw it in because of the multitude of fish; then, they realized it was the Lord. Martha was confident that if Jesus was around her brother would not die. However, when Jesus came, He told Martha, "I am the resurrection and the life. He who believes in Me, though he may die, shall live" (John 11:25).

Marian's W C dictionary defines Anxiety as, "a painful or apprehensive uneasiness of the mind over an impending anticipated ill." Whereas fear is the tool of the Devil, we overcome it by trusting in God and having confidence in Him; we must rest assured that He will never leave us nor forsake us (Heb.13:5). When I am afraid, I will trust in God because the God who promised never to leave nor forsake us is greater than the problems and has already solved them at Calvary.

The confidence in the Word and knowing Jesus' voice is the hinge to overcome fear. Jesus' comforting words to His disciples upon His departure were, "Be of good cheer. These things I have spoken to you, that in Me, you may have peace. In the world, you will have tribulation, but be of good cheer. I have overcome the world" (John 16:33).

THE FEAR OF MAN - Temptation that leads to Depression:

When Isaac went into Egypt, he was afraid that his wife would be taken from him because of her beauty. But instead of trusting God for his safety, he lied and said she was his sister (Gen.12:13, 26:7). It is better to endure trials and accept God's will than to attempt our own solutions.

CHAPTER 2:
ANXIOUS THINKING

According to Merriam Webster's College Dictionary: The definition of Fear :It is an unpleasant, often strong emotion caused by anticipation or awareness of danger.

Most people who are perplexed with fear are unbelievers or weak in faith. Christians know the Word and exercise the Word with faith instead of fear. Acknowledging God to be who He is will cast out fear. The omnipotent God, omniscient God, omnipresent God, the only true and wise God, he giveth power to the faint and those who have no might. He increases strength. He giveth wisdom. Out of this mouth comes knowledge and understanding.(Proverbs 2:6)

Sarah received strength to bear a son after she had passed child-bearing age. "And God said, 'Sarah, thy wife, shall bear thee a son indeed; and thou shall call his name Isaac; and I will establish my covenant with him for an everlasting covenant, and with his seed after him' (Gen. 17:19). Christians honor God as their burden-bearing problem solver and so cast all their cares on Him.

Some An anxiety disorder is not cured by prayer and confession only. However, people who are saved and walking in their freedom in Christ do exercise their faith in Jesus Christ as their healer. "Be anxious for nothing, but in everything, by prayer and supplication with thanksgiving, let your request be made known unto God" (Phil.4:6).

A person who has entrusted his or her life to the LORD Jesus Christ will believe God's report verses the doctor's. The doctor may give that individual six months to live, but because of the confidence and trust that person exercises in God, they will gravitate to the word of God.

A simple meaning of worry is the fear that we manufacture, and those who choose to do it certainly have a wide range of dangers to dwell upon. Whenever you give attention to the media or turn the radio on, there is something fearful or disastrous to worry about. The media is noted for telling us about those who have been exposing us to all things negative which they sensationalize however, victimized repeatedly, but the good news about the kingdom remains a secret, simply because it will not generate the views that would generate large profit margins for them. Thanks be to God who gave His son to deliver us from the fear of death and inspire us to be good moral persons of love in our communities.

There is nothing new today that was not there in the beginning. All negativity that rules the Earth today, are just a repetition of the things that have occurred before our Saviour walked the Earth. The fall of man has contributed to the fear of death unless one has made their peace with God through His son, Jesus Christ, who holds the keys of hell, death, and the grave (Rev. 1:18).

Christians' anxiety about; the turn of events and the world's nonchalant acceptance of everything evil and negative is not unfounded. Their anxiety over future generations' morality and faith in God is warranted. However, they must have faith in God and believe that He sees and knows all things. Hence, some people prepare for many things in life, but the most important thing to prepare is for the soul to meet its maker.

Therefore, thus I will do unto thee, O Israel; and because I will do this unto thee, "prepare to meet thy God, O Israel" (Amos 4:12). However, people, because of who they are, do what they do. They only cater to this life and manufacture the fear anxiety of death. If, in this life, only we have hope in Christ, we are of all men most miserable because of the enemy, death. Death is an enemy that steals our loved ones and leaves us sorrowful.

"For as in Adam all die, even so in Christ all shall be made alive" (1 Corinthians 5:20–22).

However, those of us who know Christ as LORD and Savior should not sorrow as those who have no hope. The last enemy that should be destroyed is death. Jesus, through His resurrection, conquered the power of death. So, when this corruptible shall put on the incorruption, and this mortal shall have put on immortality, and then be brought to pass the saying that is written, death is swallowed up in victory. O death, where is thy sting?

"If we receive the witness of men, the witness of God is greater; for this is the witness of God which he hath testified of His son" (1 John 5:9). By that person's faith and confidence in the healing power of God, that individual will be healed from their

anxiety both spiritually and emotionally. "When the evening [had] come, they brought unto Him many that were possessed with demons; and He cast out the spirits with His Word, and healed all that were sick." That might be fulfilled as spoken by Isaiah, the prophet, saying HE himself took our infirmities and bore our sickness (Matt. 8:16-17).

According to physiological research, fear and anxiety are the emotional or felt reactions to our perception of life events. Anxiety disorders are a life problem, and to solve them, we must consider how the person is responding to threatening events of potential disasters. Everyone handles their problems differently, especially between Christians and non-Christians. Christians have a problem solver who goes with them in their crisis. "These I have spoken unto you, that in me ye might have peace. In the world, ye shall have tribulation, but be of good cheer; I have overcome the world" (John 16:33). Therefore, Christians face their problems with confidence and faith in God to cause them to triumph over every situation life may bring their way. But unbelievers depend on the arms of flesh to help them, which fail most of the time.

The point when stress becomes distress is when external pressures put demands on our physical system, causing the adrenal gland to respond by secreting cortisone-like hormones into the physical body. However, that is as natural to the body as accepting the pressures of life. But if the pressure persists too long, our adrenal gland will act up. Where is thy sting? O grave, where is thy victory? The sting of death is sin, and the sting of sin is the law. "But thanks be to God, who giveth us the victory through our LORD Jesus Christ" (1 Cor. 15:54-57)

We all have an appointment with death, for the scripture has confirmed that: "And as it is appointed unto man once to die, [and] after this [undergo] the judgment, so Christ was once offered to bear the sins of many, and unto them that look for Him shall He appear the second time without sin unto salvation" (Heb. 9:27-28). However, freedom from this fear comes from realizing that all things, including our loved ones, belong to God. He is the God of both the dead and the living, but He does not take pleasure in the death of a sinner. God gave us this life and wants us to enjoy it while down here on earth and then present it back to Him faultless. God is a keeper and a sustainer if we should trust Him to keep us unto the Day of Judgment (Jude 24).

A wife, a husband, and children are precious to the family, but we must be able to entrust our loved ones to the care of a loving God, who gave them to us in the first place. We must realize that they were just lent to us and it behooves us to make the best of the treatment and time we invest in our families. For all the suffering, trials, and persecution the Apostle Paul had undergone, he would rather be with the LORD, but for his fellowmen, he chose to wait for the timing of the LORD to go.

Believers in the first century suffered inhumanely, in the hands of powers and wicked authorities. Some of the prophets were stoned and killed; all the apostles, except John, were beheaded for the cause of Christ.

Glands cannot keep up with that stress, and so it becomes distress, resulting in physical illness or emotional irritation. At this point, the mind has a vital part to play.

The person who has the mind of Christ will trust God for healing of both the body and the mind. "And [do] not conform to this world, but be [transformed] by the renewing of the mind, that ye may prove what is that good and acceptable and perfect will of God" (Rom. 1:2). That individual will allow the mind of Christ to dominate his mind instead of wondering about evil thoughts and things that cannot be changed, believing God for the impossible (Phil. 2:5-7).

Let this mind be in you which was also in Christ Jesus, who, being in the form of God, thought it not robbery to be equal with God. But He made Himself of no reputation and took upon Himself the form of a servant, and He was made in the likeness of men. And, being found in fashion as a man, he humbled himself and became obedient unto death even on the cross. The unbeliever will doubt and suffer distress and eventually fall apart.

A perfect example of a man of courage and confidence in God was David. Because of his heart for God, fear could not have dominion over him. He acted in faith and assurance that God would deliver the giant in his hands when everyone else's hearts failed them through fear and anxiety. According to Neil T. Anderson, "Fear is an adrenaline rush." When our minds perceive the presence of a fearsome object or being, a signal is sent from our brains to our nervous systems. When David saw the giant, he did not get afraid or anxious, but confessed confidence that "The LORD, who delivered me from the paw of the lion and from the paw of the bear, He will deliver me from the hand of this Philistine" (1 Sam 17:32-37).

They died in faith with a blessed hope and glorious assurance of eternal life (Heb. 11:3-37). Stephen, the first martyr, left a legacy for believers to follow as an example of suffering for the cause of Christ, who was forgiving and loving during his persecution. Through the power of the Holy Spirit, Stephen said, "LORD, do not hold this sin against them!" And having said this, he fell asleep (Acts 7:54-60).

If we trust God during our trials and afflictions, He will never leave us nor forsake us; assuring that we do not become anxious of the unknown. God will give us the grace to endure, for he has given more grace when the burdens grow greater. His strength is made perfect in our weakness. He is able to make all grace abound towards us. "For we have not a high priest, that [has] passed into the heavens. Jesus, the Son of God, let us hold fast our profession. Let us, therefore, come boldly unto the throne of grace that we may obtain mercy and find grace to help in the time of need."(Heb. 4:15-16).

CHAPTER 3:
CASTING ALL YOUR ANXIETY ON CHRIST

The secret of casting all your cares on Jesus is to know Him in a personal way and experiencing His mighty power. "And Jesus came and spoke unto them, saying, 'All authority is given unto Me in heaven and in earth'" (Matt. 28:17). Jesus admonished his disciples to take His yoke upon them and learn of Him, for His yoke is easy and His burden is light.

When Martha was complaining to Jesus about her sister not helping her in the kitchen, Jesus' response to Martha was that Mary had chosen the best part of serving - she was fellowshipping with Jesus and learning of Him. Paul had his testimony that he wanted to know Jesus in his fullness: "That I may know him and the power of his resurrection and the fellowship of his suffering, being made conformable unto his death. If by any means I might attain unto the resurrection of the dead..." (Phil. 3:10-11). Daniel had no doubt about his God when he challenged the king that he would not eat his food nor bow to his image because he was confident that his God would deliver him from the wrath of the king.

Living a legacy of your integrity as a steward of what God has entrusted in your care is a sign of success for a man or woman of good conduct, sincerity, truthfulness, and excellence in successful business. In the Apostle Peter's admonishment to believers, he wrote, "As obedient children, do not be conformed to the former lusts which were yours in your ignorance, but like the Holy one who called you, be holy yourselves also in your behavior, because it is written, 'You shall be holy, for I am holy.'" Who we are is far more important than what we do because who we are flows from what we do.

God gave everyone talents, skills, and abilities for His glory, but unfortunately, some use them for vain and to furnish the kingdom of Satan. However, there are those who love the LORD and acknowledge that all that we have comes from God, for all good and perfect gift comes from God.

Not everyone gets the same opportunity to utilize their skills and ability but whenever the opportunity arises those skills should be used for God's glory.

There are two kinds of failure: moral failure and failure to meet certain objectives. Moral failure cannot be blamed on anyone but ourselves. Lack of knowledge and bad decisions contribute to moral failure. Another reason for failure is sin. God is a merciful God who is faithful and just to forgive us and cleanses us from all unrighteousness (1John 1:9).

Therefore, his experience in God enabled him to motivate believers to know God, for the people who do know their God shall be strong and do exploits (Dan. 11:32).

When we know God, we believe that He will never leave us nor forsake us, for that security is sure, then we depend on Him to supply all our needs because that is what He promised. His Word is forever settled in heaven. The most basic need is spiritual life, and Jesus came so that we might have life and have it more abundantly (John 10:10). Knowing God is to identify with Christ Jesus, our savior, our high priest, our mediator, and our need supplier, and on Him we can cast all our cares. As He received glory, honor, and power, so have all His saints. (Rev. 4:11)

Peace is the opposite of anxiety; anyone who desires peace must accept the Prince of Peace, for without Jesus, "There is no peace to the wicked," sayeth God. "For the wicked is like a troubled sea when it cannot rest, whose waters cast up mire and dirt" (Isa. 57:20-21).

Anxiety is overcome by abiding in Christ and applying the Word to your life. The most important peace is the inward peace, assurance that God is potent enough to supply all your needs. But in everything, by prayer and supplication with thanksgiving, let your requests be made known to God. And the peace of God, which surpasses all understanding, shall keep your heart and your mind in Christ Jesus.

The Apostle Paul taught the believers how to overcome anxiety by deprogramming their minds. "Finally, brethren, whatever is true, whatever is honorable, whatever is right, whatever is pure, whatever is lovely, whatever is of good report, think on these things" (Phil. 4:8).

Therefore, there is no need to hide from Him. God will give you wisdom; He will lead and guide you in the right way because HE delights in the prosperity of His people.

CHAPTER 4:
THE FEAR OF MAN

Strongholds of fear are devilish; fear and discouragement are the greatest tools of the enemy. Once the Devil can get you to fear man or to be discouraged, you have lost the fight. No one should fear man more than God. It is bondage to fear man more than God. To fear God is to reverence Him. "Be not wise in thine own eyes, fear God, and depart from evil" (Prov. 3:7). Fear is a controlling spirit that should be cast out by the power of the blood of the Lamb. "The fear of man brings a snare, but he who trusts in the LORD will be exalted" (Pro. 29:25).

The stronghold must be broken by the weapon God gave us, for the weapons of our warfare are not canal, but might through God in pulling down of strongholds. "Casting down imagination and every high thing that exalteth itself above the knowledge of God, and bring into captivity every thought to the obedience of Christ" (2 Cor.10:5).

When these strongholds are broken, we can live in freedom in Christ Jesus.

For some people, it is the hardest thing and very difficult to say no. Such people are men pleasers, double-minded, driven and tossed by the winds of self-doubt and fearful of rejection, always trying to get the approval of men. These people cannot accomplish anything. James stated it this way: "A double-minded man is unstable in all his ways and is like the wave of the sea, driven with the wind and tossed. This man can receive nothing from the LORD," (James1:6).

It does not matter how hard he tries; he just cannot please everyone. The best thing to do is please God, do what is right, and satisfy you. God's strength was made perfect in Joshua's weakness; therefore he was always victorious in battle. However, at that particular time, he felt confident that he could face the enemy without the approval of God, and he made a mess; for he was defeated because he had drifted away from the fear of God to lead and guide him. (Josh. 7:13).

In Christ, we have all been allotted a measure of faith. To exercise that faith, we must have sound judgment. To accomplish the goal of complete freedom, we must take that first step in the right direction. If your plan to overcome fear includes confronting other people, it is helpful to determine in advance how you would respond to their positive or negative reactions. The plan should include parts A, B, and C. This means one must plan with options.

Many learned fears should be overcome in bite-size steps. Dr. Bourne, in his book "The Anxiety and Phobia Workbook," gives many helpful suggestions on desensitization from fears, including which includes setting realistic goals. His suggestions on how to overcome the fear of elevators will give you a clear idea indication on how this can be done.

A person who has not fully surrendered to God is most likely to seek acceptance and to identify with others. But when you are completely surrendered to God and know Him personally, not as just a God in heaven; but as your father, your friend, high priest, advocate, need supplier, burden bearer, and sufficiency, then you can say, like David, "The LORD is my shepherd; I shall not want."

People do not realize the blessings that are in fearing God and abiding in his Word. There is steadfastness:

"I will make with them an everlasting covenant, that I will not turn away from doing good to them, and I put the fear of Me in their hearts, [so] that they may not turn from Me" (Jer. 32:40).

There is friendship with God: "The friendship of the LORD is for those who fear Him," (Ps. 25:14). There is also wisdom: "The fear of the LORD is the beginning of wisdom; a good understanding has all those who practice it," (Ps. 11:10).

When you know the word of God and practice it, you will see results and not feel fearful of man, but trust in God, believing in Him for the impossible things to happen in your life. The temptation will come to cause you to struggle with the thoughts and fearful feelings, but faith in God will give you the courage to prevail.

The fear of man will cause us to lie and give in to them. However, the Apostle Paul admonished us to "lay aside the old self, which is being corrupt in accordance with the lusts of deceit, and be renewed in the spirit of your mind, and put on the new self, which in the likeness of God has been created in righteousness and holiness of the truth. Therefore, laying aside falsehood, speak the truth to one another in love, for we are members of one another" (Eph.4:22-25).

Here is a helpful prototype for making step-by-step progress toward a goal: look at elevators come and go. Stand in a stationary elevator with a trusted friend. Stand in a stationary elevator alone. Travel up or down one floor with your friend.

CHAPTER 5:
THE FEAR OF DEATH

It has been proven that nine out of ten Americans believe that the world is less safer than when they were growing up. Forty percent feel unsafe taking a walk alone at night within a half mile from home. This fear is even worst among teenagers. Forty-nine percent of teenagers in 1997 were worried about dying because of the drugs and the HIV epidemic. Now, it is even worse with guns at school and the COVID pandemic.

Young people see their peers dying every day on the curb. On the school ground, not even kindergarteners are safe from guns. According to Ernest Becker in his description of fear, "The emergence of man as we know him [is] a hyper anxious animal who constantly incents reasons for anxiety, even when there are none."

For as much, then, as the children are partakers of flesh and blood, he also likewise took part of the same himself, that through death he might destroy the one with the power of death - that is the Devil. "And deliver them, who, through fear of death, were all their lifetime subject to bondage" (Heb. 2:151).

CHAPTER 6:
THE FEAR OF FAILURE

We must recognize that fear has an object which motivates us to do something responsible or not responsible, for everyone has a different opinion of success. Some measure success by how much money you have or by how well your business is doing, stock and bonds. However, the real meaning of success must be measured by the word of God.

"This book of the law shall not depart out of thy mouth, but thou shalt meditate therein day and night, that thou mayest observe to do according to all that is written therein, for then thou shalt make thy way prosperous, and then thou shalt have good success," (Jos. 1:8-9).

We are encouraged to meditate,day and night; by doing so we are digesting the word of God. Pondering on the word will give you knowledge and revelation. Knowledge will enable you to make right decisions,strategically planning, or collaborate with likeminded people to set goals." The law of the LORD is perfect converting the soul; the Testimony of the LORD is sure, making wise the simple" (Ps. 19:7)

"The Word of God is a lamp to light our path" (Ps. 119:105). Many people study the Bible to gain knowledge. The Bible speaks for itself: "Search the scriptures, for in them, you think you have eternal life, and these are they which testify of Me. But you are not willing to come to Me that you may have life" (Hon. 5:39).

When one is walking with the LORD, the presence of God overshadows you, and the presence of fear cannot dwell in your environment. "But the Spirit of Him that raised Christ from the dead dwells in you, He that raised Christ from the dead shall also give life to your mortal bodies by His Spirit that dwelleth in you," (Rom.8:11).

When we walk in the Spirit, the fruit of the Spirit will be manifested in our lives, and the works of darkness will be cancelled.

Most healing that took place in Jesus' ministry was accomplished by faith. Jesus usually asked the sick person, "Do you believe I can do that?" Or, "What do you want me to do for you?" Jesus already knew the condition, but He wanted the person to exercise his or her faith. The only true and wise God made possible the renewal of our minds, which can be done only through His presence in our lives. Since we cannot see God, faith is the key element to the presence of God in our lives. We are saved by grace through faith. "But without faith, it is impossible to please God, for [he] that cometh to God must believe that He is a rewarder of them that diligently seek Him," (Heb. 11:6).

The entire life of the christian is contingent on Jesus, who is the way, the truth, and the life, and who unites us with God. The way we live will glorify God. The way we think to please God is by our faith. "I shall pray with the Spirit, and I shall pray with the mind also" (1 Cor. 14:15). "If you abide in Me, and My word abide in you, you shall ask what you will, and it shall be done unto you," (Jon 15:7). Therefore, by abiding in the Word of God, we will not be anxious or fearful but will live in peace and have the confidence that God will perfect the things that concerns us.

The mind is the battle ground for the enemy, for if he can destroy the mind, then he has won the battle for the soul. The minds of those struggling with anxiety and disorder can be regulated by perfect peace if the individual has the faith to keep their minds with the Word of God, for it is the peace of God that surpasses all understanding that will guard your hearts and minds in Christ Jesus (Phil. 4:7).

CHAPTER 7:
PANIC DISCOVERY

What is the meaning of panic attacks? Research has proven that about seventy-five percent of panic disorders are found in women between the ages of twenty and thirty and can first show up even in teenage years and in adults age 40.

Most panic attacks are related to stress, as stated by physiological study. It is very helpful to understand how the body works and why certain physical symptoms are necessary. Often, those symptoms are so distressing that the panic attack sufferer will believe he or she is in need of emergency medical treatment and will go to the hospital. There are genuine physical disorders that can cause symptoms that mimic a panic attack; therefore, it is wise to undergo a thorough physical examination. If a legitimate physiological reason exists, it would be wise to explore other possible causes which will enable one to get the necessary help needed. "Fear not thyself about tomorrow. HE who cares for the lilies in the field, how much more will he care for you (Matt. 10:31). There are two ways to treat Panic Attack or stress:

(1) By taking medication as ordered by your Doctor.

(2) Spiritually by feeding into the Word of God.

The Bible gives us good medicine for both the soul and the body. "For as he thinks within himself, so he is," (Prov. 23:7).

Trust in the Lord ... straight with all your heart, and do not lean on your own understanding. In all your ways, acknowledge Him, and He shall directly thy paths.

One mistake secular therapist makes is that they try to convince their clients that they are adequate in themselves to handle their panic attacks. But according to the apostles Paul,there is a difference.

"Not that we are adequate in ourselves to consider anything as coming from ourselves, but our adequacy is from God, who also made us adequate as servants of a new covenant" (2 Cor. 3:5-6).

It does not matter what the problem is; the solution is found in the word of God. "Do not be wise in your own eyes; fear the Lord and depart from evil. It will be health to your flesh and strength to your bones," (Pr. 3:7-8).

Everyone would like to have external peace at home, at work, in the community, and in the world at large. There are some people who do not like peace, although the scripture instructs us to live at peace with all men. "If possible, so far as it depends on you, be at peace with all men" (Rom. 12:18). External peace and senses of worth cannot be based on the external world because God rules in the affairs of men (Matt. 5:9).

Once people are in the world, there will always be war. James gave us an example of why there will always be war:

"From where come wars and fighting among you? Come, they not here, even of your lusts that war in your members? Ye lust, and have not, ye kill, and desire to have, and cannot obtain; ye fight and war, yet ye have not, because ye ask not. Ye ask and receive not because ye ask amiss, that ye may consume it upon your lusts," (James. 4:1-3).

For many people, anxieties are resolved by controlling those next to them, but peace will order their internal world, for the peace of God will keep the heart and mind together. Then, if you are at peace with yourself, then you can live at peace with those around you.

For some people, their wealth is their God. They spend all their lives making money, building castles, and trusting them for their security, forgetting that it is God who gave them this portion. "Every man also to whom God hath given riches and wealth, and hath given him power to eat thereof, and to take his portion and to rejoice in his labor - this is the gift of God," (Ecc.5:19).

However, one of the lessons Jesus taught was where to put your treasures, for where their treasures are, there will their hearts also be. Jesus taught that anxious people have two treasures and two visions because they are pleasing two masters, but that puts great stress on them.

"Be not wise in your own eyes; fear the LORD and turn away from evil. It will be healing to your body and refreshment to your bones" (Prov. 3:5-8). God wants us to prosper materially, but first of all, our souls must prosper as well. "Beloved, I pray that, in all respects, you may prosper and be in good health, just as your soul prospers" (3 John 1:2).

Many people chose to seek spiritual help for healing instead of medicine because of their faith in God. These people have great confidence in the Word of God because of the power of the Word. "For the word of God is living, and powerful, and sharper than any two-edged sword, piercing even to the dividing asunder of souls and spirit, and of the joints and marrow, and is a discerner of the thoughts and intents of the hearts" (Heb. 4:12).

CHAPTER 8:
BREAKING STRONGHOLDS
OF FEAR

God has not given us the spirit of fear, but most people will submit to fear instead of faith, which is the opposite of fear. If fear is not of God, then where does it come from? Fear is one of the weapons the Devil uses to torment his victims and oppress them.

They are always worrying about the future. If only they would trust God who holds the future in His hands. Anxiety comes from what you treasure in your heart and a lack of faith in God to supply your future needs (Matt. 6:19-21).

Most rich people and very poor people are likely to be anxious of the future. The rich man is worried about his wealth, how secure it is, and whether the stocks are up or down. "Thus sayeth the LORD, let not the wise man glory in his wisdom, neither let the mighty man glory in his might, let not the rich man glory in his riches" (Jer. 9:23).

The poor man is worried about where the next meal is coming from, but he needs to know that God cares for him.

"For the needy shall not always be forgotten, the expectation of the poor shall not perish forever. God created us free moral agents, free to serve Him or the Devil. However, in order for us to please God, we must die to [ourselves] and live in Christ. The plan of salvation is a complete package, consisting of deliverance, healing, reconciliation, justification, and inheritance incorporable. The

Apostle Paul puts it this way. "I am crucified with Christ, and it is no longer I that live but Christ that lives in me. And the life that I live in the flesh I live by faith in the Son of God, who loves me and gave Himself for me" (Gal. 2:20).

There is no need to worry about tomorrow if only we can bring our passion to subjection, then our material needs and our lack of faith in God. Jesus taught the disciples to overcome these things by depending on the sovereign God.

"For this reason, I say to you, do not be anxious for your life, as to what you shall eat, or what you shall drink, nor for your body, as to what you shall put on. Is not life more than food, and the body more than clothing? Look at the birds of the air. They do not sow, neither do they reap, nor gather into barns, and your heavenly Father feeds them. Are you not much more than they?" (Matt. 6:26).

Trusting God and abiding in His Word is the key solution for anxiety. Jesus bids us to cast all our cares upon Him, for He cares for us. He will perfect the things that concern us, and if we can accept that, then there will be no need to worry. "But the path of the just is like a shining light which shineth more and more unto a perfect day" (Prov. 4:18).

According to Neil T. Anderson and Rich Miller, these are some hints to overcome anxiety:

1. Go to God in prayer.

2. Resolve all known personal and spiritual conflicts.

3. State the problem.

4. Separate the facts from the assumption such as facts relating to the situation, assumptions relating to the situation and verify them.

5. Determine your active response.

6. List everything related to the situation that is your responsibility.

7. Follow through on your list of responsibilities and become accountable to someone for fulfilling your goals.

8. If you have fulfilled your responsibility and continue to walk with God in prayer, according to Philippians 4:6-8, the rest is God's responsibility.

Some people are stressed out because they won't accept the truth, nor will they come to Christ, whose ministry was to set men free. For this cause, He came, so that He might destroy the works of darkness. Jesus is the head of the Church, which is the ground and pillar of truth (1 Tim. 3:15). It is empowered by the Holy Spirit of truth (Jon. 16:13). Jesus is the only one who can give freedom and liberty to those who are in captivity.

Children are victims of fear, which is sometimes caused by growth and will be overcome by development into adulthood. In spite of age gaps, children can still be given the word for their healing (Heb. 4:12-13).

We must take into consideration that all our needs and answers to our problems are found in the Word. "I sought the LORD, and He heard me and delivered me from all my fears. They looked unto Him and were radiant, and their faces were not ashamed. The angels of the LORD encampeth round about those who fear Him and delivereth them," (Ps. 34:4).

Joshua is a perfect example for putting God first in all his planning. He sought counsel from God for strategic planning, acknowledging that God was the great counselor.

CHAPTER 9:
BUILDING A STRONGHOLD
OF FAITH

There were two men in history that we can emulate: King David and Martin Luther King Junor. Those men knew what it was to face difficult challenges of the enemy and to overcome them by taking refuge in the power of God to pull down strongholds.

What is a strong hold?

A stronghold is a well-defended place or system.

It has been said that there are two fleshly strongholds, as well as godly strongholds. Apart from Christ, we develop our own means of coping with life and defending ourselves.

Those fleshly strongholds of the mind are characterized by thoughts raised up against the knowledge of God, including doubt, unbelief, fear, and anxiety. God, however, has given us superior weapons, such as the Word, the blood, and His name. "They overcame by the blood of the Lamb and the Word of their testimony, and they love not their lives unto the death," (Rev. 12:11).

Through David's experience in life, he has written, "The LORD is a refuge for the oppressed, a stronghold in times of trouble. Those who know your name will trust in you in times of trouble. Those who know your name will put their trust in you, for you, LORD, have never forsaken those who seek you" (Ps. 9:9-10).

God is faithful. HE never allows His children to be tempted or tested beyond their ability to escape or endure (1 Cor. 10:13). Many are the afflictions of the righteous, but the LORD delivers them out of them all. The Apostle Peter knew what it was to suffer afflictions. Therefore, his testimony is a source of encouragement to us today. "But the God of grace, who hath called us unto his eternal glory by Christ Jesus, after ye have suffered a while, makes us perfect."

It takes courage to witness for Christ, especially now with so many doctrines and heresy. However, the Apostle Paul is our perfect example; in spite of all his struggles, persecutions, and trials, he was not ashamed: "I am not ashamed of the Gospel of Christ, for it is the power of God unto salvation to everyone who believeth to the Jew first, and also to the Greek" (Rom. 1:16). Paul was not ashamed because he was not a man pleaser, but a bond servant of Christ.

Most people are ashamed to share the Gospel because they value their own safety and security. The Devil hinders the propagation of the Gospel because it is for the saving of man's soul. Therefore, we should recognize that the fear comes from the Devil. "God has not given us the spirit of fear, but of power, love, and a sound mind" (2 Tim. 1:7).

When you are obedient to God, He will give you the courage to witness anywhere people are found. We must look at people with the eyes of God. Jesus saw the multitude as sheep having no shepherd, and He had compassion on them. David saw the people of God being mocked by the giant. He did not waste any time to exercise his faith in God, who had given him the courage to kill the bear, the lion, and the face of Goliath triumphantly.

It takes a higher calling to overcome the fear of man. You must consider yourself a servant of God, not man; man cannot account for your life. You are an ambassador for Christ; it is He who works in you for His good pleasure.

CHAPTER 10:
THE FEAR THAT DISPELS ALL OTHER FEARS

"For in much wisdom is much grief; and he that increaseth in knowledge, increaseth in sorrow. For wisdom is a defense, and money is a defense; but the Excellency of knowledge is that wisdom giveth life to them that have it,"

(Ecc.1:18, 7:12).

The reason why so many people are lacking knowledge is because they do not fear God; the fear of the LORD is the beginning of knowledge. God's people perish for lack of knowledge. "The fear of the LORD is the beginning of the knowledge, but fools despise wisdom and instruction. The fear of the LORD is the beginning of wisdom, and the knowledge of the Holy One is understanding" (Pro. 1:7, 9:10).

Things are possible if we can only believe. Lazarus was dead for four days, but when Jesus called him forth, he was resurrected from the dead. Jesus told Martha, "If you believe, you will see the glory of God."

The next step for deliverance from fear is repentance - a turning away from your attitude towards yourself, towards God and towards others. Or else we will meet God as judge. Worship God in sincerity. We cannot mock God. "Be not deceived, God is not mocked; whatever a man sows, that will he reap." Also, there should be reconciliation with others.

CHAPTER 11:
RECOVERING THE FEAR OF GOD

Children must be taught the fear of God at an early age by obeying and respecting their parents. The scripture admonished that they obey their parents in all things (Eph. 6:1). The Apostle John considered believers as little children of God. "Little children, let no man deceive you. He that doeth righteousness is righteous, even as he is righteous. Whosoever doeth not righteousness is not of God, neither he that loveth not his brother. Ye are Children of God, little children, and [you] have overcome them, because greater is He that is in you than he that is in the world" (John 3:7-10; 4:4).

The Apostle Paul addressed his followers as his spiritual children. He called Timothy his son. The Gospel shows how much Timothy obeyed, respected, and honored him. King David's desire was that his children emulated him by fearing and serving God. "And thou, Solomon my son, know thou the God of thy father. If thou seek him he will be found of thee, and serve him with a perfect heart and with a willing mind: for the Lord searcheth all hearts and understandeth all imaginations of the thoughts: but if thou seek him, he will be found of thee, but if thou forsake him, he will cast thee of for ever (1Chron.28:9)

The fear of God will cause us to love and serve Him. However, those who fear man instead of God have no fear of God because we must obey God rather than man, (Acts 4:19).

Acknowledgements

I AM PLEASED TO TAKE THIS OPPORTUNITY TO THANK: God whom I am most indebted to, who has given me the wisdom, and the courage to persevere to inspire me to share my influence by writing this book. All the praise and the glory goes to God for the gift and knowledge to write. I want to thank my husband pastor Julian Polidore for interceding on my behalf when I was too jaded to pray. Thanks to my colleagues, and faculty members who have helped me with this research project. I dedicated this book to my four daughters to admonish and inspire them to emulate my faith and use their influence whenever the opportunity presents itself.

Author's Biography

Dr. Joan Polidore Studied at Empire State College, worked at Holly Patterson Geriatric Center, committed servant for the Lord at Abundant Life Ministry, and served as Evangelist Dean of the Bible School. She has a Master of Divinity in Theology and ordained Chaplain of the Christian Chaplain Association of New York. Together with her husband founded Agape Ministries Inc., Christian Academy, and served as Pastor, Youth Advocate, A School Administrator and she acquired her Doctorate Degree in Christian Counseling.

CPSIA information can be obtained
at www.ICGtesting.com
Printed in the USA
LVHW051525200423
744757LV00008B/490